SEALS &
SEA LIONS

Printed in Hong Kong

98 99 00 01 02 5 4 3 2 1

Library of Congress Cataloging-in-Publication Data
Miller, David, 1959 Oct. 14–
    Seals & sea lions / David Miller.
    p.   cm. — (World life library)
    Includes bibliographical references and index.
    ISBN 0-89658-371-6
    1. Seals (Animals). 2. Sea lions. I. Title. II. Series.
QL737.P63M55   1998
599.79—dc21   97-44771
                                                CIP

Published by Voyageur Press, Inc.
123 North Second Street, P. O. Box 338, Stillwater, MN 55082 U.S.A.
612-430-2210, fax 612-430-2211

Educators, fundraisers, premium and gift buyers, publicists and marketing managers: Looking for creative products and new sales ideas? Voyageur Press books are available at special discounts when purchased in quantities, and special editions can be created to your specifications. For details contact the marketing department at 800-888-9653

SEALS &
SEA LIONS

David Miller

Voyageur Press

Contents

Introduction

Seals are among the most immediately recognisable and best loved of all wild animals, which is somewhat surprising since they spend the majority of their lives at sea, and when they come ashore they often do so in remote places out of the sight of man. Indeed, most people would recognise a seal even although they may never have seen one in the wild. Those who have seen one must have been captivated by the inquisitive, dog-like face bobbing on the surface of the sea or entranced by the beauty of a lithe animal form supremely adapted to its aquatic way of life.

It is a further intriguing aspect of the seal paradox that few animals provoke such a wide range of public opinion. Seals are thought of, on the one hand, as cute and cuddly creatures, and on the other, as marauding and voracious predators. These conflicting viewpoints are perpetuated by images of helpless pups clubbed to death on blood-covered ice, which present seals as victims of man's abuse of the environment, and by the equally emotive claims of the damage done by seals to fish stocks and the livelihoods of fishermen.

These perceptions are further complicated by man's long involvement with seals, both as resource for food, fuel and clothing, and as the root of much traditional folklore. In the 'selchie' stories of north-western Europe, seals were thought to be human women or children condemned to a life between land and sea, while in other parts of the world fishermen still consider it unlucky to kill seals because they believe that they embody the souls of dead sailors.

Much of this superstition results from the fact that although the lives of humans and seals have been closely intertwined for millennia, until recently little was known about these enigmatic creatures. It is only now, since we have been able to follow seals into their own world, that we are beginning to unravel the mysteries of their lives beneath the ocean waves and marvel at their underwater exploits.

Eared seals, like this Californian sea lion, can walk on all four limbs.

Seals and Sea Lions of the World

Seals and sea lions belong to a group of mammals related to the terrestrial carnivores (bears, dogs, cats and weasels) which is called the Pinnipedia, meaning the 'wing-footed animals' after their large paddle-shaped limbs and webbed flippers. The Pinnipeds are further divided into three families: the earless or so-called true seals (the Phocidae), the eared seals (the Otariidae), and the walruses (the Odobenidae). Although, thankfully, fewer marine mammals are now kept in captivity than in the past, the 'seal' which many people are most familiar with, the one in zoos and circuses (which balances balls and claps its fore-flippers), is likely to be a Californian sea lion which is not strictly speaking a true seal at all. In fact, it is an animal which belongs to the family Otariidae and which is truly at home in the surf off the coast of the north-eastern Pacific. These Otariids (or eared seals) include the sea lions and fur seals and they comprise 14 species around the world, although there are no representatives in the northern Atlantic. They are probably only distantly related to the true (or earless) seals or Phocidae which comprise 19 species world-wide. The harbor seal, or common seal as it is known in the British Isles, is a typical true seal.

The precise origins of seals are shrouded in the mists of time because the earliest fossil records from some 20 million years ago reveal seals which look very much like those alive today. Scientists agree that the ancestors of seals were terrestrial carnivores but they disagree about which type of carnivore gave rise to the pinnipeds and about whether they arose once or twice during the process of evolution. One theory suggests that sea lions and fur seals (the Otariids) and walruses may have evolved from a bear-like ancestor on the shores of the Pacific, while the true seals (the Phocids) arose more recently from an otter-like ancestor around the Atlantic. If this was the case, then the constraints of life in the water have resulted in these two separate groups developing a remarkably similar streamlined

A bull northern elephant seal rests on a Californian breeding beach.

body shape and physiology through a process known as convergent evolution. On the other hand, an alternative theory is that all pinnipeds arose from a similar (bear-like / otter-like) ancestor in different parts of the world at around the same time and they have subsequently developed the differences we see today.

So, as well as obvious similarities, today's true seals and eared seals exhibit important differences which make it relatively easy to tell them apart. For example, eared seals have external ear flaps, larger fore-flippers which are used to propel themselves underwater, and hind-flippers which can turn forwards allowing them to stand on 'all-fours' and walk on land. True seals, on the other hand, have no external ear flaps; they have relatively small fore-flippers and large hind-flippers, which are their main form of propulsion in the water and which cannot be turned forward, with the result that true seals on land use an apparently awkward shuffling movement to get around. Walruses, with their enormously enlarged upper canine teeth, have some of the characteristics of both groups (hind flippers which can turn forward and no external ear flaps) and are in a family by themselves. Since seal and sea lion family names are somewhat confusing I will continue throughout this book to use 'seals' to include all the Pinnipeds, 'true seals' to describe Phocids, and 'eared' seals to describe Otariids.

All seals have had to develop senses which enable them to thrive both in the water and on the land. One of the most appealing and characteristic features of all seals are the whiskers, or vibrissae, on the sides of their faces. These are important tactile organs which may, for some species at least, be essential in finding prey. The walrus, for example, has six hundred whiskers which it uses to detect invertebrate prey while feeling its way along the sea bed.

The seal's conspicuously large eyes contribute to its appealing, dog-like face. These are designed for low light conditions underwater and seals do not see particularly well on land. However, despite their large eyes and excellent vision in

A walrus uses its tusks for fighting and display, and as anchors when hauling itself onto ice.

A female Australian sea lion shows the remarkable flexibility typical of all seals. Among the rarest of seals, they are a significant tourist attraction on Kangaroo Island.

the water, blind seals have been found in the wild which were apparently healthy in other respects, proving that they are able to hunt successfully and avoid predators using touch and sound alone.

Hearing is therefore clearly important to seals in both air and water and is probably their most important sense. As well as hearing frequencies much higher than we can, they are also particularly adept at locating the source of a sound. This not only allows them to avoid potential predators, it also enables them to approach unseen prey until they are close enough to catch it by touch or sight.

Whether or not seals have a sense of taste is open to debate and difficult to prove one way or another. They tend to swallow their food whole or in large pieces without chewing so taste is likely to be relatively unimportant. Although of little use to them underwater where their nostrils are closed, seals have an acute sense of smell on land, which is vitally important when detecting predators and is also used by mothers to identify their pups on a crowded breeding beach.

Some species of true seal are relatively quiet, many others, especially those living among the ice of the polar regions, are very vocal, both on land and in the water. The sounds they make are likely to serve a variety of purposes; in particular they are used for communication between mother and pup, in territorial disputes, and possibly as a way of locating breathing holes from the water beneath the ice.

Although life in the water has dictated that seals resemble one another both in shape and physiology, they are a remarkably diverse group in many other respects. For example, they vary enormously in size. The female Galapagos fur seal is among the smallest, measuring only 4 ft 10 in (1.5 m) long and weighing around 77 lb (35 kg) – smaller than even the new-born pup of the gargantuan southern elephant seal which may weigh 88 lb (40 kg) at birth and whose adult males reach 16 ft (5 m) in length and over 3.5 tonnes in weight. Even within the same species, males and females may differ dramatically and this sexual dimorphism is at its most extreme in the sea lions where adult males may weigh three times as much as adult females.

Geographically, seals range throughout the oceans of the world; the greatest diversity of species and the largest populations occur in food-rich seas at high latitudes in both the northern and southern hemispheres. The Arctic ocean and North Atlantic are home to walruses and several species of true seal, including harps and hoods, ribbon seals, spotted seals, bearded seals, gray seals, harbor seals, and tiny ringed seals which have been recorded as far north as the Pole. The warmer oceans and seas of the world have relatively few areas which are rich enough in fish and other marine prey to support large populations of seals and indeed they are completely absent from many areas. Exceptions to this rule include the endangered Mediterranean and Hawaiian monk seals, the southern and Californian sea lions, and four species of fur seal which, in some cases, are virtually restricted to single island groups such as the Galapagos. The South Atlantic and Antarctic Oceans are particularly productive in terms of marine life and consequently they support a variety of southern seal species, often in huge numbers. Australia has its own sea lion and fur seal, New Zealand its own fur seal, and true seals of the Antarctic include the crabeater seal, Ross seal, Weddell seal, leopard seal and of course the largest of them all, the southern elephant seal.

As well as being distributed throughout the oceans of the world, seals vary considerably in the way they utilize the marine environment. Some remain relatively close inshore in shallow coastal waters and although they travel between haul-out sites, breeding grounds and feeding areas these journeys are usually relatively short. For example, harbor seals in north-east Scotland do not generally forage more than 30 miles (50 km) from their haul-out sites. On the other hand, some species make migratory journeys of great distances: northern fur seal females travel several thousand miles between their breeding beaches off Alaska and their winter feeding grounds off the coast of California. Surprisingly perhaps, not all seals live in the sea. The world's largest freshwater body, Lake Baikal in Russia, supports a population of Baikal seals over 1000 miles (1610 km) from the nearest ocean.

A two-day-old 'whitecoat' harp seal pup.

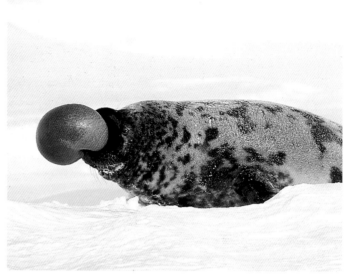

<table>
</table>

Weddell seal

Hooded seal

Bearded seal

Hawaiian monk seal

For such a small group of mammals, seals exhibit a wide diversity of habitat use and body form, which is clear from this selection of four true seals (opposite) and a typical eared seal, the New Zealand fur seal (above).

Food and Feeding

Seals exhibit considerable variety in their food preferences and while most are fish-eaters, many include cephalopods (squid and octopus) in their diet, and a few specialize on other types of prey. For example, the most abundant seal in the world, the crabeater, has an incredibly specialized diet, and relies almost exclusively on one type of prey. Despite its name, the crabeater seal in Antarctica does not eat crabs at all, instead most individuals feed exclusively on small shrimp-like crustaceans known as krill. In order to catch its tiny prey the crabeater seal has specially shaped teeth which enable it to extract the krill from a large mouthful of seawater. As the seal closes its jaws water is forced out through gaps in its teeth and the krill are trapped within the seal's mouth.

Another specialized feeder is the wonderful-looking bearded seal, which uses its fantastically long white whiskers to feel for prey (crabs and shellfish) on the sea bed along the shallow coasts of the Arctic. Its more familiar neighbor, the bizarre-looking walrus with its two spectacular tusks, also feeds on the seabed in coastal waters around the Arctic. From wear patterns on the tusks it appears that they do not actually use these for digging but instead they virtually stand on their heads underwater and disturb the sediment with their tusks while using their whiskers to find their mollusc food by touch. Once they have obtained their prey, walruses do not crush the shells; it appears they are able to exert enormous pressure to suck clams from their shells. Walruses also eat crabs, snails, shrimps, bottom-dwelling fish and, rarely, some individual walruses specialize in attacking and eating other seals.

They are not of course alone amongst the pinnipeds in eating other seals. Some sea lions also prey on the young of other seals; in Alaska, northern sea lions have been known to kill and eat as many as 6% of all the northern fur seal pups born each year. At the other end of the world the aptly named leopard seal, with its large

A leopard seal displays its massive head and jaws armed with formidable teeth.

head and jaws, specializes in taking large prey items and regularly includes penguins, and the young of other seals, in its diet. Despite their formidable appearance they also take smaller prey items including fish and cephalopods, and in some instances krill provides as large a part of their diet as penguins and seals.

Seals are not only preyed upon by other seals, some species are liable to fall prey to sharks and killer whales. Northern elephant seals on Californian beaches display spectacular scars as a result of unsuccessful great white shark attacks. Elsewhere, in colder parts of the world, a variety of seal species fall prey to killer whales. There are some spectacular photographic images of killer whales charging out of the surf to grab sea lion pups from a Patagonian beach. Killer whales in family groups also capture harbor seals off British Columbia and toss them around rather like a cat might play with a mouse before killing it. Terrestrial predators also kill seals at haul-out sites and on breeding grounds. In the Arctic, polar bears take ringed seals and hooded seals. They stalk seals on the sea ice and may lie in wait for many hours at a seal's breathing hole. When a seal emerges, the bear attempts to strike it with a paw and, if successful, will drag it from the water before eating it.

Inevitably, the subject of seal diet is highly contentious when seals come into conflict with man as a competitor for fish stocks. We know seals can dive to great depths and remain underwater for long periods of time. These skills not only enable them to efficiently exploit the food resources of the sea, they also make it extremely difficult to study their diet and foraging behavior.

Early research on seal diet was based largely on the stomach contents of seals shot near fishing nets. Not surprisingly these seals were found to be eating the types of fish caught in the nets. More recent research using less biased techniques has revealed that most seals eat a wide variety of fish as well as some cephalopods and crustaceans. Indeed, Californian sea lions are known to include over fifty species of fish and cephalopod in their diet. Most standard research techniques involve the

This Galapagos sea lion shows vivid evidence of a close encounter with a shark.

identification of prey species from hard parts, particularly distinctive fish ear bones known as otoliths, taken from the stomach contents of seals killed away from fishing nets, or from their droppings at haul-out sites. There are, of course, still biases with these techniques. For instance, two serious concerns are that small otoliths may be digested completely and therefore small fish will be under-represented, and that haul-out site samples may not be representative of fish caught at sea. More controversially, it has been suggested that if seals do not eat the head of a particularly large prey item – for example, salmon – then otoliths of that species will not be found. The abundance of small otoliths in some samples may have come from small fish in the stomachs of large cod or salmon which were subsequently eaten by seals. Techniques are being sought to overcome these difficulties and exciting new developments using molecular analysis of the predators' own tissues to detect fish-derived fatty acids may soon provide more answers. Early results from such work suggest that feeding behavior and diet may differ widely even within a single population of seals. For example, small individuals are likely to take different prey than large ones, which makes it difficult to obtain data which is representative of whole populations to accurately assess seal diet and feeding behavior.

Meanwhile, there is growing pressure from fishing industries around the world for scientists to provide answers to questions about what seals eat, where they feed, how they hunt, and how much they eat. Scientists are beginning to answer the first two questions for some species of seal, but how much they eat in their natural environment, what component of that diet would otherwise be available to man, and how they catch their prey are more difficult to assess. Even so, the general picture is that most seals are opportunistic feeders which vary their food intake and their foraging strategies to make the most of locally abundant prey. Thus their feeding behavior may differ not only from species to species but also from individual to individual, season to season, and place to place.

A northern sea lion's diet includes salmon, also prized by man, which often leads to conflict.

Life in the Water

Studying seals has never been an easy task; not only do they spend most of their lives at sea, when they do come ashore they often do so in some of the most remote and inhospitable parts of the planet. Our knowledge of seal movements around and beneath the oceans was very patchy until the 1970s when scientists began to develop recording instruments which could be harmlessly attached to seals and recovered later. Before these developments almost all information on seals was obtained from observations on land, mainly during the breeding season, or from dead animals drowned in fishing nets or killed by hunters. It is not difficult to imagine the exhilaration felt by the pioneering scientists who first fitted a simple mechanical depth recorder to a female northern fur seal in 1975 and found on her return to land that the faint trace imprinted on the paper strip represented evidence of hundreds of dives to depths of 330 ft (100 m) or more. Until that moment we could only guess what seals were doing underwater.

Today, many highly sophisticated electronic instruments are used in the pursuit of knowledge about seals and their lives in the water. These include time-depth recorders which collect data on whether a seal is in or out of the water and how fast and deep it dives or swims. These instruments or data-loggers have become so advanced that they are now small computers which can record and store a mass of information as well as simple times and depths. They can now record heart rate and other physiological data, and some are even able to take blood samples while the seal dives.

Sonic transmitters are used to track seals underwater from boats equipped with hydrophones in order to establish the shape of a dive as well as its depth and duration. Similarly, hydrophones can be used as acoustic devices to listen to the seals themselves. It is only by using such technology that we know, for example, that male

A harbor seal uses its streamlined shape to cruise effortlessly through a forest of kelp.

bearded seals emit melodic trills which are capable of traveling many miles underwater and which may be used to attract females or to defend territories. Similarly, we now know that male harbor seals also indulge in underwater vocal displays during the mating season.

VHF radio transmitters are used to track the movements of seals and because their signal can only be received when the seal is at the surface of the water or on land, they allow us to compare the amount of time seals spend in the water as opposed to the amount of time they spend hauled-out on land. These transmitters are designed to be as small as possible and have an effective range of only 12 miles (20 km) which makes them less than ideal for tracking long offshore movements. Exciting new technology has led to the development of UHF transmitters linked to data loggers which can relay information up to passing satellites. It is now possible for scientists to continuously track seals and to receive physiological data and monitor their behavior throughout the world's oceans from the comfort of their own laboratories.

However, before making use of all this advanced technology seals first have to be captured in order to attach the instruments. Almost invariably this is neither an easy nor a comfortable task and a variety of ingenious methods have been developed. Some species are relatively approachable on their breeding grounds and it is often possible to anaesthetize them from close range with tranquiliser darts from a blow pipe. Other species are not at all approachable, particularly those with pups which can swim shortly after birth, and these are often caught by a variety of rushing and netting techniques. I have experienced few things quite as exhilarating as running an inflatable boat up a beach at 25 knots and leaping out among a mass of adult harbor seals heading for the sea and man-handling them into outsize butterfly nets (without any handles). It is, of course, paramount to any valid research that the seals are not harmed by the catching process and are stressed as little as possible during data collection.

Considerable lateral thinking is also required when it comes to handling seals

Many species of seal are capable of leaping clear of the water, or 'porpoising', like this Australian sea lion. This may assist them to escape from predators, but they also probably do it because it's fun.

which may weigh several tonnes. Bull elephant seals have been encouraged on to a scaled-down weighbridge buried in the sand while following an inflatable female elephant seal being pulled on a string by an enterprising Californian researcher!

Once captured much can be learnt by taking samples of blood, tissue, milk and gut contents in ways which do no long-term harm to the seals. Blood is a particularly valuable commodity. DNA can be isolated from it, which allows research to be carried out on genetics and mating patterns. It also provides evidence of exposure to diseases and contaminants, and even insights into diet. For example, fish-induced anaemia has been detected in harbor seals.

Using techniques such as those described above, more has been learnt about seals around the world during the past two decades than was known from the previous two hundred years.

All seals are streamlined to facilitate motion through the water and they have large flippers which act as paddles and as rudders to provide the power and the maneuverability which they need both for catching mobile prey and for escaping from predators. Although wonderfully designed for movement in water this is not in itself enough for them to succeed as marine mammals; as air-breathing, warm-blooded animals, they have had to make other vital adaptations in order to thrive in an aquatic environment.

Water is a more efficient conductor of heat than air and since water temperatures encountered by seals are always lower than those of mammalian blood, seals have had to develop an array of ingenious mechanisms for reducing heat loss. These mechanisms are so efficient that some species of seal are able to live their entire lives in polar regions where the water is cold enough to kill an unprotected human within minutes.

It is no coincidence that all seals, even the smallest ringed seals, are relatively large animals with a cylindrical body shape and small appendages. This basic body shape not only aids swimming; it also provides a large inner volume where heat is generated and retained and a relatively small surface area where it is lost.

Californian sea lions migrate to and from their breeding grounds in groups or pods.

Additionally, to reduce heat loss even further, when warm blood passes from a seal's body into its flippers it has to pass through an ingenious heat exchange mechanism. Each artery (the blood vessel which carries warm blood from the heart) is enmeshed in a system of veins (blood vessels carrying cooler blood from the body surface) in order that warmth from the arteries which otherwise would be lost to the sea is instead transferred to the veins and passes back into the body. This adaptation, known as convergent evolution, is also present in whales and dolphins which face similar problems with body heat lost to cold water.

A ringed seal emerges from a crack in the ice.

Seals have also evolved sophisticated methods of insulation to further reduce heat loss. The most obvious of these is the thick coat of fur which is at its most developed in the appropriately named fur seals. As well as an outer coat of protective guard hairs they also have a particularly dense water-repellent undercoat which prevents water reaching the skin and which was in the past much sought-after by hunters. However, although fur is effective as a waterproof coat it has major drawbacks as an insulator for a diving animal. This is because as depth increases, water pressure eliminates trapped air and compresses the fur, and so reduces its heat-retaining properties.

Seals have therefore developed another type of insulation, the special layer of

Tens of thousands of harp seals gather to breed on the pack ice of the Gulf of St Lawrence.

fat known as blubber. This lies beneath the skin and cannot be compressed so it retains its value as an insulator no matter to what depth a seal dives. This layer covers the body of all seals and may reach 4 in (10 cm) or more in thickness on seals which inhabit polar regions. The blubber layer also acts as an insulator on land, enabling Weddell seals to tolerate temperatures as low as -40° F (-40° C) while hauled-out on Antarctic ice. Harbor seals in warmer temperate waters have a typical blubber thickness of up to 2.4 in (6 cm).

Seal pups do not have a fully formed blubber layer when they are born and are therefore more vulnerable to the effects of low temperatures than adults. Different species tackle this problem in different ways. To begin with most pups grow very fast and build up a blubber layer quickly. Some have a particularly dense natal fur coat and they are generally less likely to enter the water than adults. Furthermore they tend to seek shelter alongside their mothers and in the case of fur seals and sea lions the pups will often huddle together to stay warm. Ringed seals build snow lairs on sea ice in which to give birth to their pups. Not only do these protect the pup from cold and wind, they also give some protection from land predators such as polar bears and arctic foxes.

Of course, having a thick coat of blubber and fur combats the cold but it can lead to over-heating problems when the temperature rises. Fur seals and sea lions often swim together close to the surface with their large fore-flippers waving in the air to cool themselves. Elephant seals and walruses, with their gargantuan bodies, have particular problems getting rid of excess heat. Elephant seals flick sand over themselves with their flippers to keep the sun off their bare skin, and walruses expand the blood vessels under their skin which act rather like a radiator, and results in the typical striking reddish-pink color. Conversely, when walruses re-enter cold water the blood vessels under the skin contract with the result that they appear ghostly pale.

As well as keeping warm, marine mammals must be able to dive efficiently, and for this, seals have developed some quite remarkable adaptations. The simplest of

A bull gray seal reveals its characteristic flat-headed profile as it lies in a shallow pool.

Maternal care in eared seals, such as these Australian sea lions, continues for many months.

these is a muscular reflex which closes the nostrils instantly as the animal submerges. It may seem obvious, but in order to avoid breathing in or swallowing water, they have also developed a muscular reflex which automatically closes the larynx and oesophagus when they open their mouths underwater to catch prey. In order to dive as deep as their prey and spend time hunting it, seals must be able to hold their breath for extended periods. Although harbor seals only normally dive for around five minutes at a time, these dives can be repeated one after another for many hours with only short intervals at the surface between each dive. They are also capable of making much longer dives, of up to about half an hour, in extreme situations. A Weddell seal has been recorded making a dive which lasted 73 minutes, but the champion diver of the seal world, the southern elephant seal, has been recorded diving for an extraordinary two hours. When they are at sea during the several months of the non-breeding season, they may also routinely spend only five minutes on the surface between dives lasting 30 minutes each.

Contrary to what one might expect, seals do not breathe in before they dive as we would do. Taking down large volumes of air in their lungs would create difficulties with buoyancy and could lead to the 'bends' as they re-surfaced, a potentially fatal condition which affects human divers and is caused by nitrogen forming bubbles in the blood. Seals avoid these problems and achieve astonishing diving feats by breathing out before they dive and carrying the oxygen they need combined to special pigments in their blood and muscle tissue. Seals have more blood for their body size than any other mammal and it contains more of the oxygen-carrying pigment haemoglobin than ours. They also have as much as ten times the amount of oxygen-carrying myoglobin in their muscles. Additionally, their lungs are designed to collapse under pressure so what little air there is, is forced back into the windpipe from where nitrogen cannot be absorbed into the blood.

But even this is only part of the story – as well as increasing the amount of oxygen they store, seals also utilize it in a most economical way. When diving, they can reduce their heart rate to four or five beats per minute or about 10-20% of the pre-dive rate, a process known as bradycardia. This, combined with an ability to divert blood away from areas of the body where it is not needed (e.g. the liver and kidneys) and to send it to the essential organs, especially the brain, allows seals to survive very much longer dives than they would normally make. Man exhibits some of these same traits and although most people can only voluntarily hold their breath for about a minute, some individuals have survived accidental submersion in cold water for as long as half an hour by subconsciously reducing their heart rate and slowing their circulation.

Long dives may also mean deep dives and some seals are capable of reaching phenomenal depths. Harbor seals and gray seals are generally thought to feed near the seabed and are often restricted to around 160 ft (50 m) in coastal waters they inhabit. From studies it is known that they are capable of reaching depths of at least 330 ft (100 m). However, they have a long way to go to challenge the real champions of the seal diving world. Weddell seals are capable of dives to almost 2000 ft (600 m) under the Antarctic ice and even this astonishing figure has recently been exceeded by a northern bull elephant seal which was recorded diving to depths in excess of 4900 ft (1500 m) in the Pacific, which is probably deeper than some whales dive.

Not only do seals dive deep, they can also dive fast. Fur seals weighing only 88 lb (40 kg) can descend to 660 ft (200 m) and return in less than five minutes. This incredible diving ability also develops early: recent research has revealed that bearded seal pups less than a week old can dive for more than five minutes to depths of 250 ft (75 m), a skill which has probably evolved as a means of escaping polar bears. In short, although cumbersome and ungainly on land, seals are phenomenal athletes in the water.

A group of northern sea lions in the water off Round Island, Alaska.

The Breeding Cycle

Although seals are highly adapted to their aquatic way of life, there are still aspects of their life cycle for which they have to come ashore. The annual moult is one such event and it is of crucial importance because a seal's skin and fur are essential for waterproofing and temperature control. The true seals, such as harbor seals, moult their fur relatively quickly about one month after the breeding season. At this time of year some seals spend a particularly large amount of time ashore and spend little or no time feeding, but the reasons for this are not entirely clear. The most likely explanation is that by staying ashore they minimize heat loss and maintain a relatively high skin temperature which encourages blood flow close to the skin, thus accelerating the moulting process.

In elephant seals and monk seals the moult is particularly dramatic and both skin and hair are shed in large patches. This can cause irritation which southern elephant seals alleviate by wallowing in mud. In fur seals and sea lions the moult is a considerably less intrusive process which may be spread over several months. Seals spend varying periods hauled-out at other times of year for reasons entirely unconnected with moulting or breeding but the purpose for this is not known. Contrary to popular belief they are not simply basking in the sun because seals in temperate regions haul-out regularly even on the coldest winter days, and seals in polar regions remain hauled-out on ice despite the most ferocious storms.

There are clearly good reasons why seals haul-out on to land (or ice) where they are most vulnerable to predators. The prime reason that seals come ashore during the annual cycle is the need to breed out of the water. In this they differ fundamentally from the whales and dolphins which mate, give birth and suckle their young underwater. Despite the fact that some seals mate in the water, and that some pups can swim almost immediately they are born, they all come ashore to

A harp seal pup resplendent in its natal fur coat or lanugo.

give birth and to suckle their young. Female seals generally bear only one pup each year, probably because the pups have to be relatively large to survive in cold water but also because even a single pup makes enormous nutritional demands on its mother even though the period of suckling and maternal care may be incredibly short. Indeed, the shortest period of any mammal belongs to female hooded seals on the Arctic pack ice which suckle their pups for an astonishingly short four days!

Such short lactation times and correspondingly high pup growth rates are possible because seal milk is the richest of any mammal's and has a consistency like mayonnaise. Seal milk may contain as much as 69% fat and 10% protein compared with equivalent values of 3.5% fat and 1% protein for human milk. Harp seals' milk is about ten times richer in fat than cow's milk and on this diet it is not surprising that a baby seal is one of the fastest growing of all mammals. At two weeks old a harp seal pup may be over four times its birth weight. In effect they grow at a rate of 5 lb 8 oz (2.5 kg) per day and by the time suckling has finished, after only 12 days, the pup will weigh over 66 lb (30 kg), 60% of which are blubber and skin.

Breeding strategies are yet another area in which seals demonstrate great variety in a relatively small group of mammals. Seals are distributed throughout the oceans of the world and accordingly their breeding sites vary enormously. Animals can be found breeding on small ice floes in the Arctic, remote rocky islands off Alaska, sandy estuaries in north-west Europe, tropical shores on Hawaii, arid beaches in South Africa and Australia, and on the frozen Antarctic mainland.

In some species of true seal, for example bearded seals in the Arctic, females give birth to their pups in conditions of relative solitude. In others, typically the eared seals such as the northern fur seal, animals congregate in colonies of many thousands and spend several months of each year rearing their young. In contrast to the four-day suckling period of hooded seals, Galapagos sea lion pups may suckle for up to a year.

Two bull southern elephant seals fight for dominance over a section of breeding beach.

A bull northern fur seal defends a harem of much smaller females in a breeding rookery on a boulder beach in the Pribilof Islands, Alaska.

Even the two species of true seal which live in temperate waters of the northern Atlantic have markedly different breeding strategies. Gray seals pup in the autumn and winter when the females gather, often in very large numbers, at traditional breeding sites. These are usually remote, uninhabited islands often with sandy beaches, although they will breed on secluded boulder beaches and in caves on the coasts of larger land masses. In the Gulf of St Lawrence they give birth to their pups on pack ice. They come ashore before giving birth and, in complete contrast to harbor seals, remain ashore for the entire three weeks it takes to wean their pups. When born the pups weigh from 20 to 30 lb (11 kg to 14 kg) and they are covered in a thick white coat which provides insulation on land but becomes waterlogged if the pup enters the sea. The pups grow rapidly and at the end of the lactation period, which lasts only about 18 days, they will have trebled in weight. Conversely, the mothers, who do not re-enter the water or feed at this time, may lose over one-third of their body weight. The pups are then abandoned, lose their white coats and must learn to fend for themselves.

Once lactation has finished, the females become sexually receptive and mate with a nearby male. Male gray seals come ashore when the females are pupping and during lactation they use their large body size to threaten and to fight with each other to establish dominance. The dominant males then defend harems of between two and ten females against other males. Large size is important to male gray seals, not only because it enables them to win fights, but also because it allows them to spend a long time ashore without feeding. Gray seals thus exhibit clear sexual dimorphism and males may weigh two to three times as much as females. Male and female harbor seals on the other hand are similar in size which suggests that male harbor seals have a quite different mating strategy in which size is not so important.

Unusually, harbor seals breed at quite different seasons around the world with pupping occurring in every month from January to October. In California, pupping begins in late March and peaks in May, but as one progresses up the western seaboard of the USA and Canada pupping occurs later, with pups as late as

September in British Columbia. Further north pupping begins earlier again, typically May and June in Alaska, which is also the peak period in the western Atlantic around Nova Scotia. In British and European waters the main pupping season is about June.

Whatever the geographical location, and whatever the time of year, the behavior of harbor seals during the breeding season is generally the same. Females come ashore on inter-tidal sand-banks or rocks to give birth. Although small and vulnerable when first born the pups are more advanced at this stage than those of most other types of seal. They have already shed their first white coat, or lanugo, in their mother's uterus and are able to swim and dive within their first hour. At this tender age they are, in fact, the best adapted of all seals to their watery environment and it is this which enables harbor seals to breed in areas disturbed by humans, whereas gray seals are more restricted in their choice of breeding sites. Indeed, the harbor seal is the most widespread of all seals, occurring on both sides of the Atlantic, in the Arctic and around the rim of the North Pacific.

Harbor seal lactation lasts for three to four weeks during which time the pup more than doubles in weight on the rich milk. In the early days, mother and pup remain close and tend to haul-out together on each low tide. The mothers probably spend little time feeding and may lose considerable weight. As weaning approaches the mothers make longer feeding trips but it is unclear whether pups accompany them or wait for their return. After weaning the pup must fend for itself, surviving on its fat reserves until it is able to catch its own prey. Like other true seals, females become sexually receptive at the end of lactation but in contrast to most other seals mating takes place in the water and not on land.

As in almost all other seals a two- to five-month period of delayed implantation then follows, while the fertilized egg floats around the uterus, before implantation in the uterine wall enables development of the embryo to continue. This mechanism allows the pregnancy to last approximately twelve months and enables the pups to

Twinning in seals is exceptionally rare; they have never been known to survive to weaning.

The bond between mother and pup is very strong. A female northern sea lion must be able to recognize her pup when she returns to the breeding colony after a feeding trip.

be born at the same time every year despite the fact that the gestation period generally lasts only seven to nine months. During the rest of the year females feed intensively, building up their blubber layer, to provide the fat reserves necessary for the next breeding season.

Like gray seals, northern elephant seals gather in large numbers at traditional beaches to breed. Females arrive between December and March and give birth about a week after hauling-out. The pups are then suckled for almost a month until they are weaned. The females then become sexually receptive so throughout this period males are engaged in vigorous competition for females. Much of the obvious aggression is channelled into vocal threats and displays and dominance hierarchies are established which reduce the need for actual fighting. However, inevitably some fighting does occur, particularly when two seemingly evenly matched males refuse to back down as a result of the mutual threat process. When they occur, pitched battles are very spectacular and can be quite ferocious, although the thick skin and blubber around the bulls' necks reduces the risk of serious damage.

Like the breeding cycles of these true seals, the lives of eared seals revolves around the yearly breeding season and for northern fur seals this begins in late spring when the Arctic sea ice retreats. At this time, northern fur seals congregate in vast numbers on traditional breeding islands which are transformed from empty beaches to become arenas for some of the most dramatic gatherings of animals anywhere in the world. One such breeding area is the Pribilof Islands off the coast of Alaska where hundreds of thousands of fur seals gather to breed in colonies, called rookeries, each year. Older bulls clamber on to the rocky shores first and set up breeding territories from which they exclude other less dominant males. They are splendid animals, 6 ft (2 m) long and weighing over 550 lb (250 kg), with thick fur coats and short manes, and they are in peak condition after a winter spent feeding further south on squid and fish. They need to be in top condition because they will now spend two months ashore without food or rest. Throughout the summer bulls vie for the best positions on the beach, usually at the edge of the sea, and control areas which may be only a few square yards in extent. Boundary disputes are normally settled by ceremonial threat behavior without the need for fighting which uses a great deal of energy and carries risk of injury to both protagonists. Threats are likely to involve roaring, staring sideways and lunging, and often the smaller or less aggressive will turn away to avoid physical confrontation.

Female northern fur seals arrive at their breeding sites in June having spent the winter further south than the males. They tend to return to exactly the same part of the beach they used the previous year, and for many this will be the site of their own birth. Soon they will outnumber the bulls by as many as 40 to one. After only a day or two ashore they give birth to a single pup and for the first week or so the mother stays with the pup, suckling it and providing it with protection and shelter. In marked contrast to true seals, the female fur seal now returns to the sea for seven to ten days of fishing followed by two days of nursing, a pattern which will be repeated throughout the summer. The pups meanwhile gather in large crèches and will spend the summer with thousands of other pups on the breeding beaches or in the shallow waters immediately offshore. This is a hazardous time for them, as they are at risk from being crushed to death by careless bulls and endangered by storms, sharks and killer whales. After four hectic months, as the short summer ends, breeding activity ceases and the beaches begin to empty. At this time the seals moult and the pups are weaned. The females head south again on a 3000-mile (4828-km) journey which will take them to their winter quarters. The pups are left behind and eventually they too will head out to sea in search of food.

Provided they survive the dangers of their first year, most seals are relatively long-lived, attaining 20 years or more. Exceptionally, a female gray seal reached 46 years. Since most seals die at sea the major causes of death are not well understood. Disease, parasitic infection, pollution, drowning in fishing nets, and predation are all known causes of mortality.

Seen packed together, it is easy to forget that elephant seals came perilously close to extinction.

Man, Seals and Sea Lions

Although nature conservation is a relatively recent concept, man has been concerned with seals for a very long time. In fact, seal remains have been found in archaeological sites dating back several thousand years and it seems likely that seals would have fallen victim to hunter-gatherers from an early stage in man's evolution. A seal would have been a most valuable quarry and would have provided meat for food, blubber for fuel, and a skin for clothing and shelter. In the Arctic until recent times the very survival of native peoples was dependent on seals and seal products. Such indigenous people can justifiably be viewed as original nature conservationists – people who viewed the environment with respect, were an integral part of it, and by necessity utilised its resources in a sustainable way.

This type of subsistence hunting made relatively little impact on seal populations for many thousands of years but all that changed with the advent of hunting for trade in the eighteenth century. Facilitated by the development of fast sailing vessels and, later, steamships which enabled global commerce, many species of seal, together with the great whales, were exploited on a vast scale by hunters from Europe and North America. Millions of northern fur seals were slaughtered off Alaska, and northern elephant seals were reduced to a world population of fewer than a hundred by 1890. Elephant seals were largely exploited for oil which was extracted from their blubber whereas fur seals were killed for their skins. This trade was so lucrative that the revenue from northern fur seal skins alone reputedly equalled the $7,200,000 purchase price of Alaska in only six years of exploitation.

In the early part of the twentieth century the killing of Californian and northern sea lions continued off the western seaboard of the USA, both for commercial exploitation and for fishery protection. They, together with northern elephant seals, northern fur seals, harbor seals and gray seals, now receive varying degrees of

Southern elephant seals at Husvik, South Georgia, site of past exploitation of marine mammals.

protection in the USA under the Marine Mammal Protection Act and other legislation. Due to legal protection populations of all species have recovered from past exploitation and none now faces extinction. The period of unregulated seal killing around the world ended when populations became so small they were no longer profitable to hunt. Fortunately this happened before the last individuals were killed and only one species is known to have become extinct in historical times.

Hunting, albeit on a smaller scale, still goes on, but the motives are often less clear and the hunts themselves can be surrounded by controversy. Some are still carried out by indigenous people in the Arctic and while this may be acceptable to preserve their unique seal-dependent culture it is not certain if these hunts remain sustainable. Methods of traveling and killing have changed from the relatively inefficient and traditional use of kayaks and harpoons to the far more efficient and modern use of skidoos and rifles.

Considerably more questionable are hunts around the developed world which are justified on the grounds that they are required to preserve fish stocks, and that they utilize a marine resource on a sustainable basis. Species which are the subject of ongoing culls include Cape fur seals in Namibia and harp seals in Canada. The controversial harp seal cull was banned in the late 1980s amid a world-wide public outcry, but it has since re-opened on the basis of questionable total population figures and claims from fishermen that the seals are hindering the recovery of an indefinitely closed cod fishery off Newfoundland. There is a widely held belief among marine scientists and conservationists that re-opening the harp seal cull had more to do with political expediency than with a coherent fisheries policy. A European ban on white-coat pup pelts is still in force and there is little world-wide demand for seal products with the notable exception of the Far Eastern market where various seal parts are sold as aphrodisiacs. In 1996, the entire quota of 250,000 harp seals was obtained within a month and the continued cull has led to calls for

The grace and agility of the majestic sea lion can be truly appreciated when seen underwater.

boycotts of Canadian fish in Western Europe. Despite this, the total allowable catch for harp seals was increased to 275,000 in 1997.

Seal hunting around the British Isles has never occurred on such a huge scale, but even so it was sufficient to reduce the gray seal population to a reported 500 individuals in 1914. This led to the Gray Seal Protection Act, the first time a British mammal (other than a game animal) had been protected by law. The hunting of harbor seals for their fur continued until the 1960s and the introduction of the Conservation of Seals Act. Since protection, seals have recovered and recent increases in populations have brought them into conflict with fishermen. Britain now supports 50% of the world's gray seals and is, in a sense, the guardian of this species.

Seals conflict with fishing interests in three ways. Firstly, seals damage nets and fish within them; secondly, seals eat fish which fishermen could otherwise catch; and thirdly, seals act as hosts to parasites which also affect fish. The direct effect of seals on fishing nets and the fish within them is an age-old problem at coastal netting stations and more recently at fish farms, where nets are fixed and which seals learn to associate with an abundant food supply. Despite general

Discarded fishing gear kills seals.

protection around the world, legislation often allows seals to be shot at or close to fishing gear and such shooting is likely to increase as conflict grows alongside increasing seal populations and numbers of fish farms. While many would argue that

Walruses gather together during the non-breeding season and seek physical contact.

seals should be completely protected it is undeniable that seals can cause great economic damage in often marginal rural communities and such local control has no effect on overall seal populations.

However, wholesale reductions in seal numbers, as has been suggested by many fishing interests, is morally unacceptable to a considerable number of people and in any case, there is no scientific evidence to suggest that it would reduce levels of damage. It seems likely that damage to fixed nets is largely caused by a small number of rogue seals, specialist individuals which learn to associate nets with food. It would be better to concentrate our ingenuity and resources on developing and deploying more effective anti-predator nets or acoustic scaring devices.

Seals also affect fisheries indirectly by eating fish in the open sea, which fishermen argue, they could otherwise catch. In areas of the world where seals are abundant they undoubtedly eat a great many fish, but there is little evidence to suggest that reducing seal numbers would actually increase the fish caught in commercial fisheries. Marine ecosystems are highly complex and despite scientific analysis and computer modelling the effects of a massive seal cull are impossible to predict with any degree of confidence.

Seals act as hosts for marine nematode worms which also infect fish. Although these worms do not pose a health risk to humans (they are killed when fish are frozen or cooked) they undoubtedly reduce the value of fish and an increase in codworm infestation around Canada and Norway has been linked to increases in gray seals. Around the world the argument between fishing interests and conservationists is becoming increasingly polarized as fisheries decline and scapegoats are sought. When fishermen search for the causes of dwindling fish stocks they rarely think to look in the mirror. Too often the debate on seal diet and interactions with fishermen is reduced to a simplistic level whereby assessments of food intake by captive seals are merely extrapolated. Recently, a fisheries minister announced that

Increasing numbers of Antarctic fur seals may damage fragile vegetation and soils.

The crabeater seal is a creature of the Antarctic pack ice. It is by far the most common seal and earns the accolade of the world's most abundant large mammal.

while it had been estimated that seals in British waters could account for 250,000 tonnes of fish per year it was not possible to draw direct comparisons with landings from fishing fleets, as seals mostly ate species not consumed by humans. Indeed, research has shown that at certain times of the year tiny sandeels comprise over 60% by weight of the diet of harbor and gray seals.

Furthermore, and somewhat contradictory, the British government has gone on to announce that although it will not sanction a seal cull as demanded by fishermen, an alternative means of controlling seal numbers should be found. The most obvious alternative to culling seals in order to control their numbers is the use of contraceptive vaccines, which stimulate the immune system to inhibit the functioning of sperm or eggs, thereby rendering an animal infertile.

It is of course a big question whether or not seal populations should be controlled at all. Many would argue it is man's activities that need to be managed and our population which needs to be controlled, that it is unethical to interfere with the reproduction of wild animals, and that fertility control is just another example of man's inappropriate attempts to manage nature. On the other hand if one accepts that it is legitimate to control seal numbers then controlling fertility has potential advantages over other methods. Advocates would argue that it is humane, potentially very effective and can be species specific. There seems little doubt that if control of seal numbers has to be carried out at all, then the use of fertility should be considered. However, at present the vaccination has to be delivered individually by injection and a great deal of further research and development is required before a practical option is found for remote seal breeding sites.

It is worth emphasizing that we simply do not know enough about the marine ecosystem to blame seals for problems which we ourselves may have created. For example, in South Georgia, one of the subantarctic islands, a fur seal population explosion is thought to be partly due to increased supplies of krill following the demise of whales at the hand of man. Here, as in many other parts of the world, seal populations previously hunted to near extinction are now expanding rapidly, causing extensive destruction to vegetation, and soil erosion at breeding sites.

A notable exception to the rule that seals have done well this century are the monk seals. The three species of monk seal are considered to be the most primitive of seals and are unusual in that they are limited to warmer parts of the world. The Caribbean monk seal was last seen in 1952 and is almost certainly extinct, the Hawaiian monk seal is endangered but appears to be less at risk than the Mediterranean monk seal which has been described as one of the world's ten most endangered mammals. Hunted since earliest times for local use, the monk seal only became threatened during the nineteenth century when large-scale commercial hunting began. Once numbers became low, hunting for skins ceased but populations have not recovered. In recent years monk seals have continued to decline as fisheries have failed, food has become scarce and seals have been persecuted by fishermen. At the same time coastal development and mass tourism have driven seals from their favored breeding beaches to rocky shores and caves. The total world population has been estimated at around 500 with half in the Mediterranean and half in the Atlantic; more may exist in an area between Western Sahara and Mauritania, but this is difficult to survey because of a border dispute. However, in the summer of 1997, mortality of disastrous proportions struck this area and an estimated two hundred animals died. Initial research has laid the blame on highly toxic dinoflagellate algae which contain neurotoxins which can pass to seals through the marine food-chain. Similar chemicals found in so-called 'red tides' have previously been implicated in the mass deaths of marine mammals elsewhere.

Interest in seals in Britain perhaps reached a peak during the phocine distemper virus outbreak in 1988. The disease affected both gray and harbor seals but particularly harbor seals with some 18,000 dying in Europe, 3000 of them around the British Isles. Much scientific and media interest surrounded the epidemic and although a previously unidentified virus was discovered to be ultimately responsible, aspects of the disease are still not fully understood. It appears to have been the natural occurrence of a type of disease which has affected other seals in other

Harbor seals have the widest world distribution, but are less numerous than crabeater seals.

places, and which may have affected European seals in the past. So, although in this case a man-made calamity was probably not responsible, the massive public interest highlighted the concern people feel about the future of the oceans. Over-fishing, sewerage discharge, oil pollution and waste disposal are just some of the threats facing seals and other marine life today.

Crude oil is the most conspicuous form of marine pollution and causes severe damage, particularly to seabirds, which rely on their feathers for insulation. The effects on seals are less dramatic because, unlike seabirds, they do not preen and ingest the oil so readily. They also largely rely on their blubber rather than their fur for insulation and so do not suffer from exposure when coated with oil. However, as predators situated near the top of the marine food-chain seals consume other pollutants which undoubtedly do affect them. Heavy metals, particularly mercury, occur at high levels in many species of seal but without apparent adverse effects. Polychlorinated biphenyls (PCBs) are highly toxic, fat-soluble chemicals which have been found at high levels in seal blubber and mother's milk. These by-products of the plastics industry have been linked with reproductive failure and increased rates of disease in gray seals in the Baltic and harbor seals in the Netherlands.

Elsewhere there are other worrying signs that all is not well in our oceans: in the Gulf of Alaska harbor seal numbers more than halved between 1984 and 1992, while northern sea lion numbers have dropped by 75% since the 1960s. Despite research a clear-cut cause has not been forthcoming; food shortages seem to be the most likely explanation but whether declines in fish stocks are a result of natural changes to the marine ecosystem, or have been caused by over-fishing or global warming, is unknown.

In contrast to many other wild creatures, many seal populations appear to be thriving, but their long-term future lies with us. The destruction of the seemingly limitless oceans through abuse and neglect could yet be mankind's ultimate folly.

In some areas, particularly the Baltic, gray seals suffer from the effects of pollution.

Enjoying Seals and Sea Lions

There can be few more enjoyable experiences in the natural world than to sit on a rocky cliff above a boulder beach on a rare sunny autumn day when the air is still and the sea a tranquil blue. A tumbling raven flies by, croaking, and the weird, melancholy wail of a gray seal drifts upwards. It is so strange, almost unnatural, that when first heard it is difficult to believe it belongs to this world, more likely the next. Seals can be frustrating animals to watch: often it is only possible to catch a brief glimpse of an inquisitive head which pops up apparently to inspect us or our passing, or they appear as little more than specks hauled-out in the distance.

For those lucky enough to dive with them, in their own environment, the grace and beauty of these wonderfully adapted creatures can be truly appreciated. The consummate ease with which they twist and turn within their three-dimensional world is a humbling experience for the lumbering human diver. For those keen to see seals at close quarters and not fortunate enough to dive, there are a number of options. Some people will be lucky enough to live in parts of the world, for example Scotland or California, where seals are common and very conspicuous. It is all too easy for those who live in these areas to take seals for granted and not realise how privileged they are to share their coastline with them. It is always a great pleasure to witness the excitement and delight the fleeting glimpse of a seal can give to visitors from areas with no seals around their own coasts.

As opportunities around the world for whale watching have grown in recent years so, rather more quietly, have opportunities for seal watching. There are now all-inclusive trips on board ships which cruise to some of the world's most remote places, including the Arctic and Antarctic. Tourists can now experience the astonishing excitement of seal colonies which were previously the exclusive preserves of hunters and scientists. Rather more accessible are seal-watching trips

A Galapagos Islands sea lion rests between feeding trips.

by boat from many harbors in north-west Europe, North America and elsewhere. In a few places it is even possible to take part in organised trips to breeding beaches. One of the most spectacular of these is at Ano Nuevo in California where the sight, sound and sheer earth-shaking power of battling bull elephant seals rivals any other experience I have had in the animal world. In the same area and almost as impressive are the sea lions – *lobos marinos* – or sea wolves, with their distinctive barking and habit of lounging on marina wharves and jetties, much to the annoyance of boat owners.

A white-coated gray seal pup.

Although not an advocate for keeping marine mammals in captivity there is no doubt that genuinely orphaned or injured seals reared in captivity at appropriate marine life centres can be a huge attraction and they offer a wonderful resource for environmental education. Captive animals also present excellent opportunities for research into aspects of seal biology and behavior which are still not possible in the wild, even with the help of today's advanced technology.

When watching seals, care should be taken not to cause disturbance, particularly at breeding sites where this may result in females deserting their pups. Never forget that seals and sea lions are wild animals and getting too close could result in you getting crushed or bitten. It is better to use binoculars and a telephoto lens to view and photograph from a distance safe for both the viewer and the seals.

A female gray seal is alert and wary when ashore.

Seals & Sea Lion Facts

Common Name	Scientific Name	Distribution	Diet / Prey	Average Length ♂ / ♀	Average Weight ♂ / ♀	Estimated World Population
EARED SEALS						
Northern sea lion (Steller's sea lion)	Eumetopias jubatus	North Pacific	Mainly fish & squid. Occasionally young seals	2.8 / 2.2m 9.2 / 7.2ft	600 / 270kg 1323 / 595lb	250,000
Californian sea lion (includes Galapagos sea lion)	Zalophus californianus	California & the Galapagos	Mainly cephalopods, some fish	2.4 / 1.8m 7.9 / 5.9ft	300 / 100kg 661 / 221lb	160,000
South American sea lion (Southern sea lion)	Otaria byronia	Atlantic & Pacific coasts of S America	Mainly squid & crustaceans, occasionally penguins & young fur seals	2.3 / 1.8m 7.5 / 5.9ft	300 / 140kg 661 / 309lb	300,000
Australian sea lion	Neophoca cinerea	Australia	Fish & squid	2.3 / 1.5m 7.5 / 4.9ft	250 / 80kg 551 / 176lb	2–5000
New Zealand sea lion (Hooker's sea lion)	Phocarctos hookeri	New Zealand	Fish, cephalopods, crustaceans & penguins	2.5 / 1.8m 8.2 / 5.9ft	300 / 100kg 661 / 221lb	5000
Gaudalupe fur seal	Arctocephalus townsendi	Mexico	Squid & fish	1.8 / 1.2m 5.9 / 3.9ft	140 / 50kg 309 / 110lb	500–1000
Galapagos fur seal	Arctocephalus galapagoensis	Galapagos Islands	Fish	1.5 / 1.2m 4.9 / 3.9ft	60 / 35kg 132 / 77lb	5000+
Juan Fernandez fur seal	Arctocephalus philippii	Chile	Cephalopods & fish	2 / 1.5m 6.6 / 4.9ft	160 / 60kg 353 / 132lb	6000
South American fur seal	Arctocephalus australis	Atlantic & Pacific coasts of S Am.	Cephalopods, crustaceans & fish	1.9 / 1.4m 3.2 / 4.6ft	160 / 50kg 353 / 110lb	350,000
Subantarctic fur seal	Arctocephalus tropicalis	Subantarctic islands	Squid, fish & krill	1.8 / 1.4m 5.9 / 4.6ft	140 / 40kg 309 / 88lb	270,000
Antarctic fur seal	Arctocephalus gazella	Subantarctic islands	Mainly krill. Some fish & squid	1.9 / 1.3m 6.2 / 4.3ft	180 / 40kg 397 / 88lb	1.8 m

Common Name	Scientific Name	Distribution	Diet / Prey	Average Length ♂ / ♀	Average Weight ♂ / ♀	Estimated World Population
Cape fur seal (South African or Australian fur seal)	*Arctocephalus pusillus*	SW Africa & Australia	Fish & cephalopods	2.1 / 1.6m 6.9 / 5.2ft	250 / 60kg 551 / 132lb	1.4 m
New Zealand fur seal	*Arctocephalus forsteri*	New Zealand	Cephalopods & fish	2 / 1.5m 6.6 / 4.9ft	180 / 50kg 197 / 110lb	20,000
Northern fur seal	*Callorhinus ursinus*	N Pacific	Mainly fish	2.1 / 1.4m 6.9 / 4.6ft	250 / 50kg 551 / 110lb	1.8 m

WALRUS

Common Name	Scientific Name	Distribution	Diet / Prey	Average Length ♂ / ♀	Average Weight ♂ / ♀	Estimated World Population
Walrus	*Odobenus rosmarus*	Arctic Ocean	Mainly molluscs	3.2 / 2.6m 10.5 / 8.5ft	1200 / 800kg 2646 / 1764lb	250,000

TRUE SEALS

Common Name	Scientific Name	Distribution	Diet / Prey	Average Length ♂ / ♀	Average Weight ♂ / ♀	Estimated World Population
Ribbon Seal	*Phoca fasciata*	Pacific Arctic	Fish, crustaceans & cephalopods	1.6 / 1.6m 5.2 / 5.2ft	90 / 90kg 198 / 198lb	240,000
Ringed seal	*Phoca hispida*	Arctic & Baltic	Fish & crustaceans	1.5 / 1.4m 4.9 / 4.6ft	80kg / 60kg 176 / 132lb	3.5–6m
Caspian seal	*Phoca caspica*	Caspian Sea	Small fish & crustaceans	1.4 / 1.4m 4.6 / 4.6ft	60 / 60kg 132 / 132lb	500,000+
Harp seal (Greenland seal)	*Phoca groenlandica*	Arctic	Fish & crustaceans	1.7 / 1.7m 5.6 / 5.6ft	130 / 130kg 287 / 287lb	2.6–3.8 m
Spotted seal (Larga seal)	*Phoca largha*	N Pacific & Arctic	Fish, crustaceans & cephalopods	1.6 / 1.5m 5.2 / 4.9ft	90 / 80kg 198 / 176lb	400,000
Harbor seal (Common seal)	*Phoca vitulina*	N Atlantic, Arctic & Pacific	Mainly fish	1.7 / 1.6m 5.6 / 5.2ft	110 / 80kg 361 / 176lb	500,000
Baikal seal	*Phoca sibirica*	Lake Baikal	Freshwater fish	1.3 / 1.3m 4.3 / 4.3ft	70 / 70kg 154 / 154lb	60,000
Gray seal	*Halichoerus grypus*	N Atlantic & Baltic	Mainly fish	2 / 1.8m 6.6 / 5.9ft	230 / 150kg 507 / 331lb	215,000
Hooded seal	*Cystophora cristata*	NW Atlantic & Arctic	Fish & squid	2.5 / 2.2m 8.2 / 7.2ft	300 / 200kg 661 / 441lb	300,000

Common Name	Scientific Name	Distribution	Diet / Prey	Average Length ♂ / ♀	Average Weight ♂ / ♀	Estimated World Population
Bearded seal	*Erignathus barbatus*	Arctic & subarctic	Molluscs, crustaceans & fish	2.3 / 2.3m 7.5 / 7.5ft	250 / 250kg 551 / 551lb	600,000– 1m
Mediterranean Monk seal	*Monachus monachus*	Mediterranean & W Atlantic	Fish & octopus	2.5 / 2.5m 8.2 / 8.2ft	260 / 260kg 573 / 573lb	500
Caribbean Monk seal	*Monachus tropicalis*	Caribbean				Extinct
Hawaiian Monk seal	*Monachus schauinslandi*	Hawaiian Islands	Fish & cephalopods	2.1 / 2.3m 6.9 / 7.5ft	170 / 250kg 375 / 551lb	500–1000
Crabeater seal	*Lobodon carcinophagus*	Antarctica	Mainly krill	2.3 / 2.3m 7.5 / 7.5ft	220 / 220kg 485 / 485lb	16–35 m
Leopard seal	*Hydrurga leptonyx*	Antarctica & sub-antarctic islands	Krill, young seals, penguins & fish	2.8 / 2.9m 9.2 / 9.5ft	320 / 370kg 706 / 816lb	200,000
Weddell seal	*Leptonychotes weddellii*	Antarctica	Mainly fish	2.8 / 3.3m 9.2 / 10.8ft	400 / 500kg 882 / 1102lb	250,000+
Ross seal	*Ommatophoca rossii*	Antarctica	Mainly squid	2 / 2.3m 6.6 / 7.5ft	210 / 200kg 463 / 441lb	200,000
Southern Elephant seal	*Mirounga leonina*	Subantarctic islands	Mainly squid	4.9 / 2.8m 16 / 9.2ft	4000 / 800kg 8818 / 1764lb	600,000
Northern Elephant seal	*Mirounga angustirostris*	NE Pacific	Mainly squid (& fish)	4 / 3m 13.1 / 9.8ft	2000 / 600kg 4409 / 1323lb	115,000

Seals vary in size depending on age, geograhical location and time of year. Weights and lengths given are typical averages for adults. Estimating seal population sizes is generally extremely difficult given their wide-ranging marine lifestyles. Population estimates vary in accuracy depending on the species involved, the counting technique used and the date of the most recent census. Figures given should be considered only as estimates.

Index

*Entries in **bold** indicate pictures*

Recommended Reading

There are many excellent books available which provide more information on the lives of seals and sea lions. These include:

Anderson, S., *Seals*, Whittet Books, (1990)
Bonner, W.M., *The Natural History of Seals*, Christopher Helm, (1989)
Bonner, W.M., *Seals and Sea Lions of the World*, Blandford, (1994)

King, J.E., *Seals of the World*, Oxford University Press, (1983)
Reeves, R.R., Stewart, B.S. *Seals and Sirenians*, Sierra Club Books and Leatherwood, S. (1992)
Thompson, P. M., *The Common Seal*, Shire Natural History, (1989)

Biographical Note

David Miller graduated with a zoology degree from the University of Edinburgh and is now a nature conservationist by profession. He currently works for Scottish Natural Heritage as Reserves Manager for Beinn Eighe and Loch Maree Islands National Nature Reserves in the north-west of Scotland. Prior to that he was Reserve Warden for the Isle of Rum National Nature Reserve off the west coast of Scotland and before that he worked for the University of Aberdeen on a research project investigating the ecology and behavior of harbor seals in the Moray Firth, north-east Scotland. He has also worked on other nature reserves with resident seal populations, including the remote island archipelago of St Kilda, best known for its huge seabird colonies, which once supported the British Isles' most isolated human population. He has held a life-long fascination with islands and the sea, has traveled widely, and has studied seals and other wildlife in various parts of Europe and North America.